EUROPE

ASIA

AFRICA

PACIFIC OCEAN

INDIAN OCEAN

AUSTRALIA

To young paleontologists past, present, and future

Special thanks to Carl Mehling of the Department of Paleontology, The American Museum of Natural History, New York, New York; Kenneth Angielczyk, Ph.D., of the Integrative Research Center, The Field Museum, Chicago, Illinois; and Alexander Clark, Ph.D. Candidate, University of Chicago, Integrative Research Center at the Field Museum for reviewing the text.

The Library of Congress has catalogued the
first edition as follows:
Gibbons, Gail.
Dinosaur discoveries / by Gail Gibbons.
p. cm.
ISBN 0-8234-1971-1 (hardcover)
1. Dinosaurs—Juvenile literature. I. Title.
QE861.5.G53 2005
567.9—dc22
2004060701

Third Edition
ISBN: 978-0-8234-5864-6 (hardcover)

AUTHOR'S NOTE

This book is about dinosaurs that lived on land long ago. Some dinosaurs evolved into birds, and the earliest birds lived alongside other dinosaurs. This book focuses on non-bird dinosaurs, the last of which disappeared about 66 million years ago. These creatures shared the planet with other animals and sea life. Scientists piece together what they think dinosaurs looked like from fossils that are millions of years old. Along with fossils, scientists now have some specimens of the soft tissues of dinosaurs, including feathers, skin, and even digestive tracts. Scientists also use comparisons with living animals to make educated guesses about what dinosaurs were like.

Besides birds, crocodiles are the closest living relatives of dinosaurs. Different dinosaurs had certain features that resemble birds or crocodiles. For example, some dinosaurs had feathers like birds, but others had scaly skin and bony armor plates on their backs, something like a crocodile. Dinosaurs also laid eggs, just like birds and crocodiles do today.

Very few of all dinosaur fossils in existence have been uncovered. Scientists continue to find exciting new dinosaur fossils, which help us learn new things about the lives of dinosaurs. Studying the world of dinosaurs will always be a process of discovery.

DINOSAUR
DISCOVERIES

By **GAIL GIBBONS**

HOLIDAY HOUSE · NEW YORK

BOOM!

A catalclysmic event happened 66 million years ago. The theory is that a giant meteorite blasted an enormous crater into Earth's surface. Most scientists think the impact and the following events caused the end of the dinosaurs. The impact of the object raised millions of tons of dust, dirt, and sand into the atmosphere. Skies darkened, blocking out sunlight. Volcanoes erupted, and there were earthquakes and tidal waves. Almost all plants died from lack of sunlight. Earth became a cold, dark place, where almost everything died. Today, scientists refer to it as the end of the Age of the Dinosaurs.

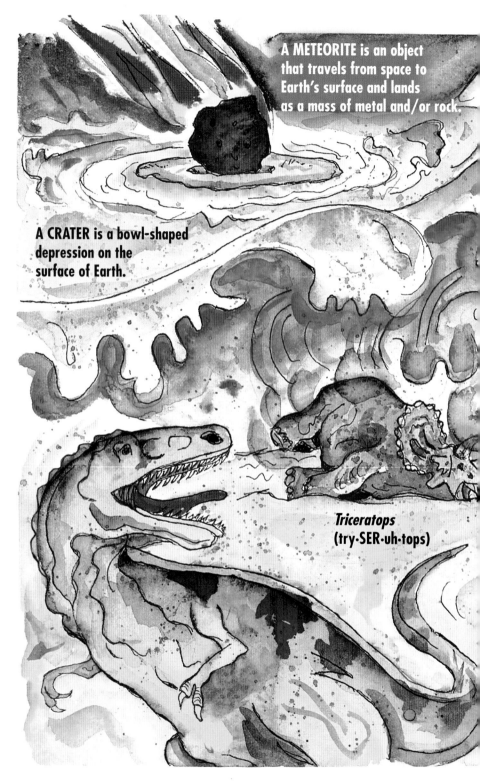

A METEORITE is an object that travels from space to Earth's surface and lands as a mass of metal and/or rock.

A CRATER is a bowl-shaped depression on the surface of Earth.

Triceratops
(try·SER·uh·tops)

Dinosaurs died off, but some smaller animals were able to survive such a disaster. Life went on.

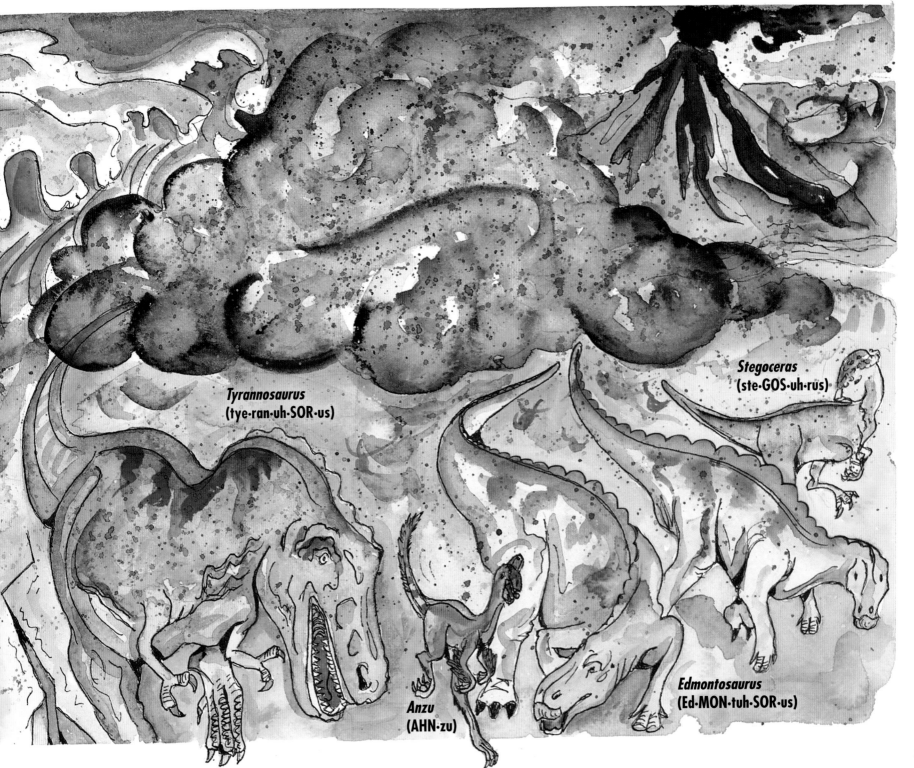

Tyrannosaurus
(tye·ran·uh·SOR·us)

Stegoceras
(ste·GOS·uh·rus)

Anzu
(AHN·zu)

Edmontosaurus
(Ed·MON·tuh·SOR·us)

3

The CENOZOIC ERA
(sen·oh·ZOH·ik)
was after dinosaurs lived.

The MESOZOIC ERA
(mez·oh·ZOH·ik)
was when dinosaurs lived.

An ERA is one of three main divisions of geologic time.

A PERIOD is a part of an ERA.

CRETACEOUS PERIOD

CRETACEOUS (krih·TAY·shus) PERIOD
145 to 66 million years ago

Ankylosaurus
(ang·kie·lo·SOR·us)

Protoceratops
(pro·toh·SER·rah·tops)

Some dinosaurs were gentle creatures and others were fierce attackers. Some were meat eaters, but most were plant eaters. They survived for 165 million years, between 230 and 66 million years ago. But the only way we know dinosaurs existed is because of the discovery of dinosaur fossils.

JURASSIC (jeh·RASS·ik) PERIOD
201 to 145 million years ago

Kentrosaurus
(ken·tro·SOR·us)

JURASSIC PERIOD

TRIASSIC PERIOD

TRIASSIC (try·ASS·ik) PERIOD
252 to 201 million years ago

Mussaurus
(mus·SOR·us)

The PALEOZOIC ERA
(pay·lee·oh·ZOH·ik)
was before dinosaurs lived.

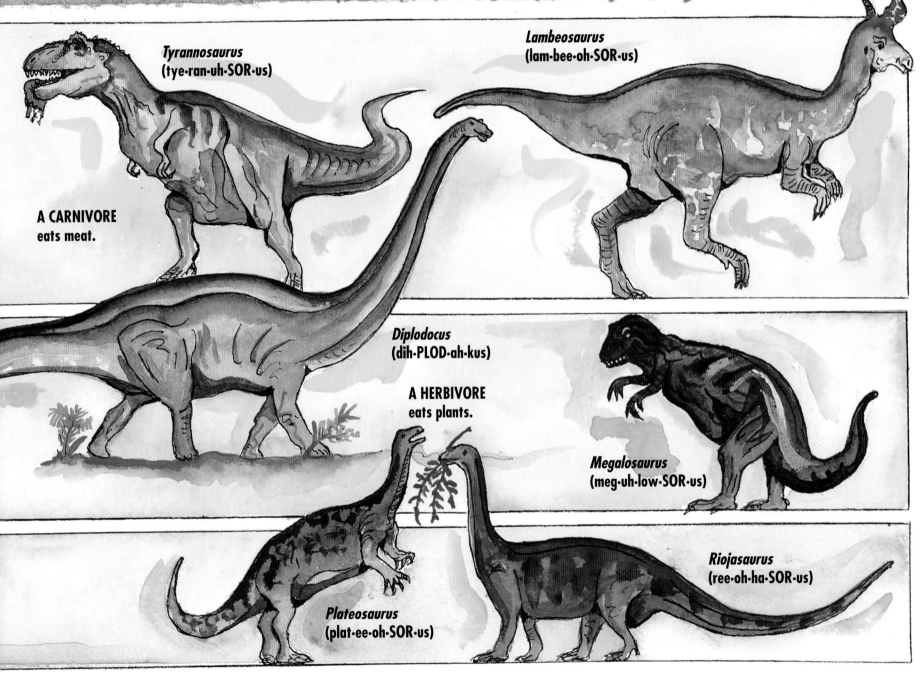

Tyrannosaurus
(tye·ran·uh·SOR·us)

Lambeosaurus
(lam·bee·oh·SOR·us)

A CARNIVORE
eats meat.

Diplodocus
(dih·PLOD·ah·kus)

A HERBIVORE
eats plants.

Megalosaurus
(meg·uh·low·SOR·us)

Plateosaurus
(plat·ee·oh·SOR·us)

Riojasaurus
(ree·oh·ha·SOR·us)

The first fossils scientists determined to be those of a dinosaur were discovered in England in the 1820s. Dinosaurs died millions of years ago, and over time, sand, mud, and other materials covered them. Over many, many years, the bones of the dinosaurs turned into fossils. Dinosaur fossils have been found lying on the ground or embedded in earth or rock. Many dinosaur fossils have been found by amateurs, sometimes by accident. Other fossils have been found by paleontologists.

In 1842, Sir Richard Owen, a scientist, named the creatures whose fossils he was studying *dinosaurs*, which means "terrible lizard" in Greek.

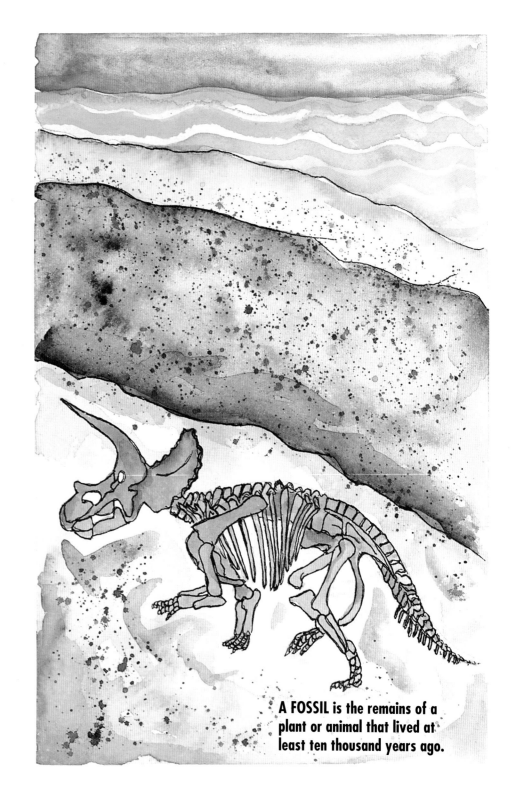

A FOSSIL is the remains of a plant or animal that lived at least ten thousand years ago.

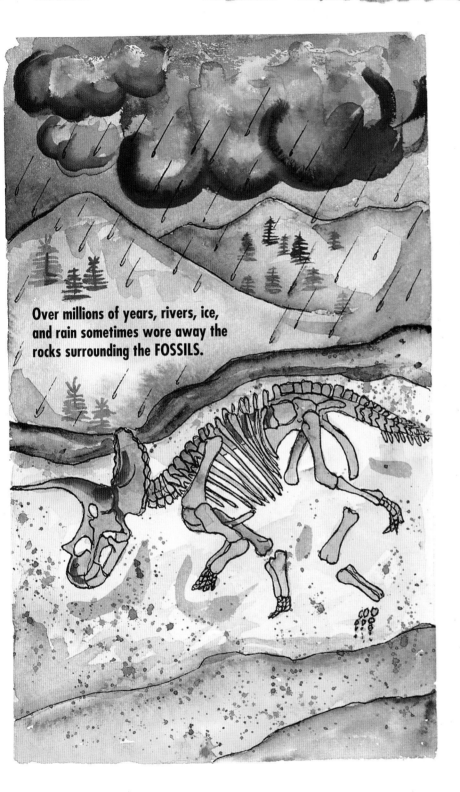

Over millions of years, rivers, ice, and rain sometimes wore away the rocks surrounding the FOSSILS.

A PALEONTOLOGIST (pay·lee·on·TOL·o·jist) is a scientist who learns about ancient life by studying fossils.

The discovery of a dinosaur fossil is often an important event. Who knows? With each find, a new kind of dinosaur could be discovered. After the paleontologists arrive at the site, they record the date, time, and place of the find. Next, excavation begins. Fragile fossils, big and small, are removed using special tools. The fossils are sent to a laboratory or museum, where they are further cleaned and studied, and the reconstruction of a dinosaur begins. The fossilized bones are assembled like pieces of a puzzle. Broken fossils are glued together using an adhesive. Next, people attempt to re-create missing pieces, muscle placement, and layers of skin, trying to figure out what the dinosaur looked like. From discovery to reconstruction can take years.

Natural history museums often have reconstructed dinosaur skeletons on display.

HAMMERS

CHISELS

POWER CHISEL

PICKS

BRUSHES

SHOVELS

POWER DRILL

About one thousand different kinds of dinosaurs have been discovered so far. When a new kind of dinosaur is found, it is usually given a Latin or Greek name that describes what it looked like, or it is named after a person who found it or the place where it was found.

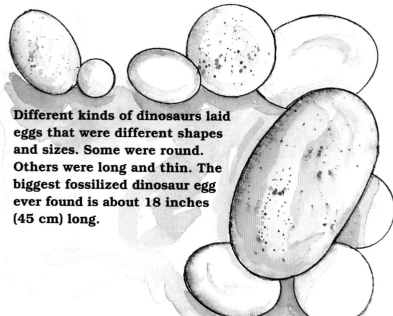

Different kinds of dinosaurs laid eggs that were different shapes and sizes. Some were round. Others were long and thin. The biggest fossilized dinosaur egg ever found is about 18 inches (45 cm) long.

PROSAUROPODS

(pro·SOR·uh·pods) were one of the earliest groups of dinosaurs.

Paleontologists have classified dinosaurs into different groups based on what their bones looked like. One of the earliest groups, prosauropods, lived during the Triassic Period. Most of them walked on all four legs. They had lizardlike heads, long necks, big bodies, and long tails. Prosauropods ate plants. Some of these early dinosaurs could stand on their hind legs to reach for leaves and branches on trees or to run from enemies.

TRIASSIC

Riojasaurus (ree·oh·ha·SOR·us) means "Rioja lizard." The dinosaur was named after La Rioja province in Argentina where it was found. It was about 33 feet (10 m) long.

Anchisaurus (ang·kee·SOR·us) means "near lizard." The dinosaur was named this because it lived near the beginning of the Age of the Dinosaurs.

Anchisaurus was about the size of a large dog

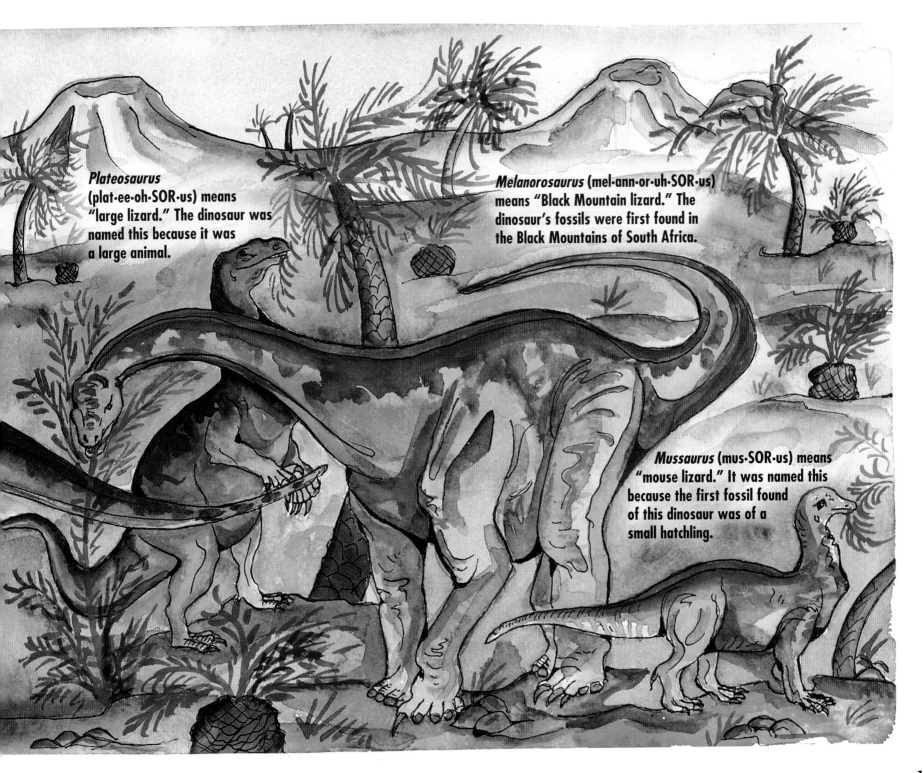

Plateosaurus (plat·ee·oh·SOR·us) means "large lizard." The dinosaur was named this because it was a large animal.

Melanorosaurus (mel·ann·or·uh·SOR·us) means "Black Mountain lizard." The dinosaur's fossils were first found in the Black Mountains of South Africa.

Mussaurus (mus·SOR·us) means "mouse lizard." It was named this because the first fossil found of this dinosaur was of a small hatchling.

THEROPODS

(THEH·ruh·pods) were the group of meat-eating dinosaurs.

Theropods are another group of dinosaurs. All of these creatures stood on powerful legs. They had claws on their toes. When running, their long and stiff tails counterbalanced the weight of their huge heads and bodies. Most of them used their very sharp claws and powerful jaws to kill and eat their prey. Some theropods were small, fast hunters with sickle-shaped claws on their hind legs.

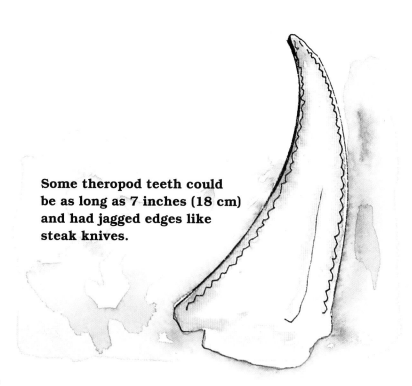

Some theropod teeth could be as long as 7 inches (18 cm) and had jagged edges like steak knives.

JURASSIC

Dilophosaurus (die·low·foh·SOR·us) means "two-crest lizard." The dinosaur was named this because it had two bony ridges on its head.

Megalosaurus (meg·ah·low·SOR·us) means "big lizard." The dinosaur was named this because it was huge.

Compsognathus (komp·sog·NAY·thus) means "elegant jaw." The dinosaur was named this because the first fossils found were beautifully preserved.

Giganotosaurus (jih·ga·note·oh·SOR·us) means "giant southern lizard." The dinosaur was named this because it was a giant dinosaur and was found in South America. It was about 46 feet (14 m) long.

Deinonychus (die·NON·uh·kus) means "terrible claw." The dinosaur was named this because both of its feet had large hooked claws.

Tyrannosaurus (tye·ran·uh·SOR·us) means "tyrant lizard." The dinosaur was named this because it was a terrifying dinosaur. It is sometimes called *Tyrannosaurus rex. Rex* means "king" in Latin.

Velociraptor (vuh·loss·uh·RAP·tor) means "swift robber." The dinosaur was named this because it could run fast.

Ornithomimus (or·nih·THOH·mih·mus) means "ostrich mimic." The dinosaur was named this because some parts of the skeleton resemble modern birds.

15

SAUROPODS

(SOR·o·pods) were the largest of all dinosaurs. They were long-necked plant eaters.

Sauropods were the tallest and largest of all dinosaurs. They moved about on four legs that supported their enormous weight. They held their long tails off the ground to counterbalance their long necks. Some sauropods grazed in herds for protection. When predators appeared, some sauropods may have used their whiplike tails like a bat to make a loud, cracking sound to scare away their enemies.

JURASSIC

Camarasaurus (cam·uh·ruh·SOR·us) means "chambered lizard." The dinosaur was named this because its vertebrae had air spaces, or chambers, in them.

Brachiosaurus (brack·ee·oh·SOR·us) means "arm lizard." The dinosaur was named this because of its long front legs.

Apatosaurus (a·pat·oh·SOR·us) means "fraud lizard." The dinosaur was named this because some of its bones deceptively looked like those of another dinosaur.

Argentinosaurus was possibly the heaviest creature to have ever walked on land. It weighed as much as 100 tons (90 tonnes).

Diplodocus (dih·PLOD·ah·kus) means "double beamed." The dinosaur was named this because of the double row of bones inside its tail.

16

Saltasaurus (salt·ah·SOR·us) means "Salta lizard." The dinosaur was named after Salta province in Argentina where it was found.

Argentinosaurus (are·jen·teen·oh·SOR·us) means "Argentina lizard." The dinosaur was named for Argentina where it was found. It was about 98 feet (30 m) long.

STEGOSAURS

(STEG·uh·sors) were the group of plated dinosaurs.

Stegosaurs had plates and spikes on their backs and tails. Some paleontologists think the plates were used to attract mates and scare off any rivals. Stegosaurs ate plants. When attacked, they may have swung their spiked tails at their enemies.

JURASSIC

PLATES

SPIKE

Kentrosaurus had both plates and spikes on its back.

Stegosaurus (steg·uh·SOR·us) means "roof lizard." Paleontologists first thought that the plates laid flat on the dinosaur's back, forming a "roof." It was about 30 feet (9 m) long.

Kentrosaurus (ken·tro·SOR·us) means "spiked lizard." The dinosaur was named this because it had so many spikes.

Wuerhosaurus (woo·err·ho·SOR·us) means "Wuerho lizard." The dinosaur was named for Wuerho, a town in China, where it was found.

ANKYLOSAURS

(ang·kie·lo·SORS) were the group of armored dinosaurs.

Ankylosaurs were heavily armored for protection, both from predators and in battles for mates. Their bodies were covered with thick plates. Some ankylosaurs had spikes and some had strong tailbones with bony clubs on their ends. These creatures could swing their tails to whack any attackers. They ate plants.

Saichania (sye·CHAN·ee·uh) means "beautiful." The dinosaur was named this because its fossils were unusally fine specimens when they were found.

The CLUB at the end of the tail had two rounded bony sides, often as big as basketballs.

Euoplocephalus (you·op·low·SEF·ah·lus) means "well-protected head." The dinosaur was named this because it had a heavily protected bony skull.

20

Polacanthus (pole-ah-CAN-thus) means "many spikes." It is believed this dinosaur had many rows of spikes on its back.

Pinacosaurus (pin-ak-o-SOR-us) means "broad lizard." The dinosaur was named this because of the bony, plank-like armor on its skull.

Hylaeosaurus (high-lay-uh-SOR-us) means "forest lizard." The dinosaur was named this because it was found in a wooded area of England.

Ankylosaurus (ang-kie-lo-SOR-us) means "stiffened lizard." The dinosaur was named this because of its fused, bony armor. This dinosaur was about 33 feet (10 m) long.

21

CERATOPSIANS

(ser·ra·TOP·see·uns) were the group of dinosaurs often having large horns and heads with frills.

Ceratopsians had bony frills on the backs of their heads. Some had three horns, and some had only two. Their horns were used as weapons. They were plant eaters that broke off plants for food using their strong beaks. It is believed some lived in herds.

CRETACEOUS

Pachyrhinosaurus (pack·ee·rine·oh·SOR·us) means "thick-nose lizard." The dinosaur was named this because it had a thick, massive bone on its nose.

Pentaceratops (pen·tuh·SER·uh·tops) means "five-horn face." The dinosaur was named this because it can look like there are five horns on its face.

Torosaurus had the largest skull of any land animal that ever lived. Its skull was about 8 feet (2.4 m) long.

22

Torosaurus (tor·uh·SOR·us) means "pierced lizard." The dinosaur was named this because there were two large holes in the frill part of its skull.

Protoceratops (pro·tuh·SER·rah·rops) means "first-horned face." The dinosaur was named this because it was believed to be closely related to the first ceratopsian.

HORN

FRILL

Triceratops (try·SER·ah·tops) means "three-horn face." The dinosaur was named this because it had three horns on its head. This animal was about 30 feet (9 m) long.

23

ORNITHOPODS

(OR·nih·thuh·pods) were the group of dinosaurs that usually had beaks or bills.

Ornithopods, which were plant eaters, used their beaks or bills to rip and tear their food. Some had extremely thick skulls with many small bumps and horns. Some ornithopods had unusually shaped crests on their heads. Some had birdlike feet and stood on their hind legs most of the time. Some walked on all fours. Paleontologists believe some of these dinosaurs lived in herds.

JURASSIC

BEAK

Dryosaurus (dry·oh·SOR·us) means "oak lizard." The dinosaur was named this because it lived among trees. It was about 13 feet (4 m) long.

Lesothosaurus (less·oh·tho·SOR·us) was named for Lesotho, the country in southern Africa where it was found.

Edmontosaurus (ed·mon·to·SOR·us) means "Edmonton lizard." The dinosaur was named this because its fossils were first found near the city of Edmonton in Canada.

Lambeosaurus (lam·bee·oh·SOR·us) was named after Lawrence Lambe, a famous paleontologist. It had a head crest.

BILL

CREST

Corythosaurus (koe·rith·uh·SOR·us) means "Corinthian helmet lizard." The dinosaur was named this because its crest looked like a Greek Corinthian helmet.

Parasaurolophus (para·saw·ruh·LOAF·us) means "near crest." The dinosaur was named this because the long curved crest on its head was similar to that on another dinosaur called *Saurolophus* (saw·ruh·LOAF·us)

Hypsilophodon (hip·see·LOAF·uh·don) means "Hipsilophus lizard." The dinosaur was named this because its teeth resembled the teeth of a lizard named *Hipsilophus* (hip·see·LOAF·us).

25

Paleontologists believe dinosaurs had keen senses of sight, smell, and hearing. Most had eyes on either side of their heads so they could see all around them, but some, like *Tyrannosaurus*, had eyes that faced forward, improving their depth perception. Their ears were holes behind their eyes. They were constantly on the lookout for food or for the possibility of being attacked. Some paleontologists believe the crested ornithopods could communicate with sound. The crests were hollow and were part of the airway inside their noses. When the crested ornithopods blew air through the airway, they might have been able to honk, bellow, or make trumpet sounds.

Paleontologists think a *Tyrannosaurus* could smell its prey and anything else from a great distance.

NOSTRIL

Parasaurolophus
(para·saw·ruh·LOAF·us)

CREST

NOSE

MOUTH

EAR

AIRWAY

Most female dinosaurs probably laid their eggs in soft, dirt nests. Some sat on their eggs, keeping them warm until they hatched. Other dinosaur mothers carefully covered their eggs for protection with plants, sand, and dirt, creating small mounds. The coverings also kept the eggs warm. When the eggs hatched, many kinds of hatchlings could live on their own right away. Still other dinosaur mothers took care of their young until the hatchlings were strong enough to live on their own.

In the 1920s, the first fossilized dinosaur nests were discovered in the Gobi Desert, in Mongolia, by an expedition from The American Museum of Nautal History in New York City.

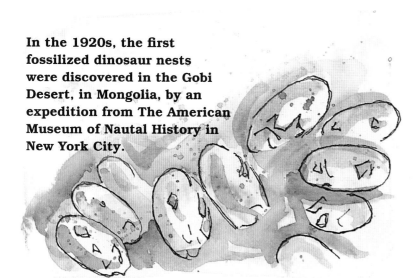

NESTS

EGGS

Maiasaura (my-ah-SOR-ah) means "good mother lizard." The dinosaur was named this because the first fossils found were near a nest of hatchlings, suggesting it cared for its young. It was an ornithopod.

MOUND

HATCHLINGS

Birds are a subgroup of theropod dinosaurs, which means that birds are living dinosaurs. *Archaeopteryx* (ark·ay·OP·ter·ix), an early bird, was a theropod that lived about 150 million years ago. It had sharp teeth. Its arms were covered with feathers, forming broad wings. Some scientists think certain types of scales evolved into feathers. Current evidence suggests that over millions of years, these feathered dinosaurs evolved into the birds we know today.

Dinosaur discoveries . . . new ones are always happening.

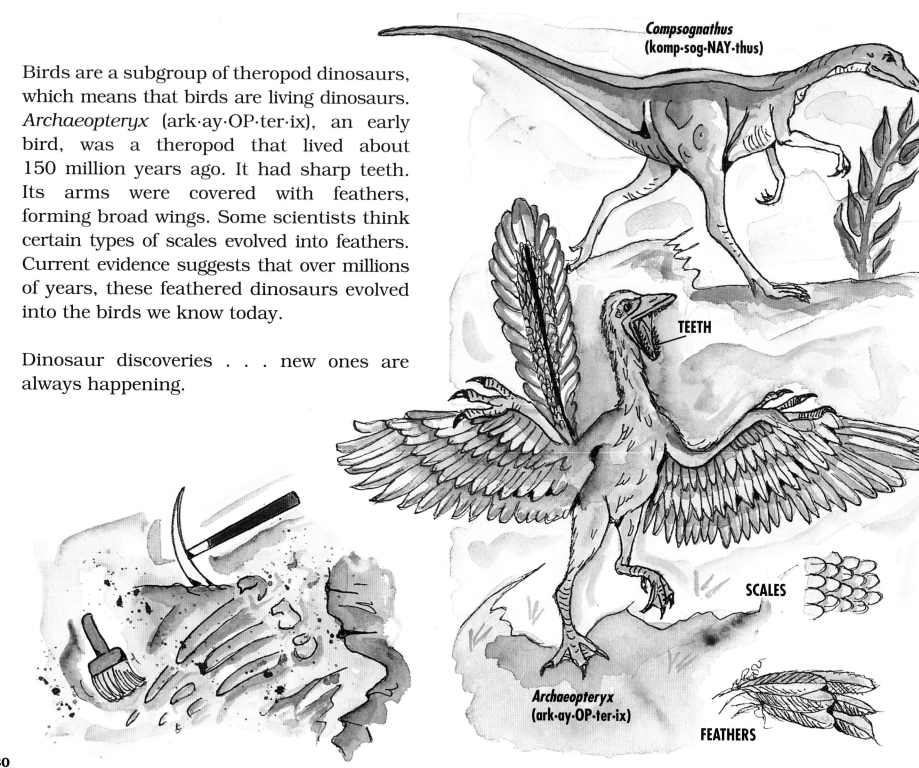

Compsognathus
(komp·sog·NAY·thus)

TEETH

SCALES

Archaeopteryx
(ark·ay·OP·ter·ix)

FEATHERS

OSTRICH

WHOOPING CRANE

NORTHERN
CARDINAL

BLUE JAY

SPARROW

MORE DINOSAUR DISCOVERIES

Compsognathus (komp·sog·NAY·thus), a theropod, was one of the smallest dinosaurs. It was only about 3 feet (1 m) long.

Coelophysis (seel·oh·FIE·sis), a theropod, may have eaten its own kind. Fossilized *Coelophysis* skeletons have been found with *Coelophysis* bones inside them.

Argentinosaurus (ar·jen·TEEN·oh·SOR·us), a sauropod, is thought to be the longest dinosaur that ever lived. It is estimated that it could grow up to 130 feet (39.6 m) long.

The largest skeleton of a *Tyrannosaurus* (tye·ran·uh·SOR·us), a theropod, ever to be found was 42 feet (12.6 m) long. It was discovered in South Dakota by a woman named Sue Hendrickson, so the fossilized skeleton was named Sue. It is on display at the Field Museum in Chicago, Illinois.

Gallimimus (gal·ee·MY·mus), a theropod, may have been the fastest running dinosaur. It is thought it could run about 40 miles (64 km) an hour.

Mamenchisaurus (mah·men·chi·SOR·us), a sauropod, is thought to have had the longest neck of any dinosaur, about 49 feet (14.7 m) long.

Dinosaurs that ate meat had very different-looking teeth than plant-eating dinosaurs. Those that ate meat usually had curved, blade-sharp teeth with sawlike edges. The plant eaters' teeth were leaf-shaped and not as sharp.

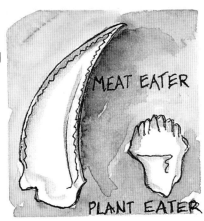

MEAT EATER

PLANT EATER

Titanosaurus (tie·tann·oh·SOR·us), a sauropod, left fossilized footprints about 3 feet (.91 m) wide. The footprints are big enough to sit in.

Eoraptor (EE·oh·rap·tor) means "dawn robber." *Eoraptor* lived at the beginning of the dinosaur era. A hunting dinosaur was often called a robber. *Eoraptor* is one of the oldest dinosaurs ever discovered.

DINOSAUR INDEX

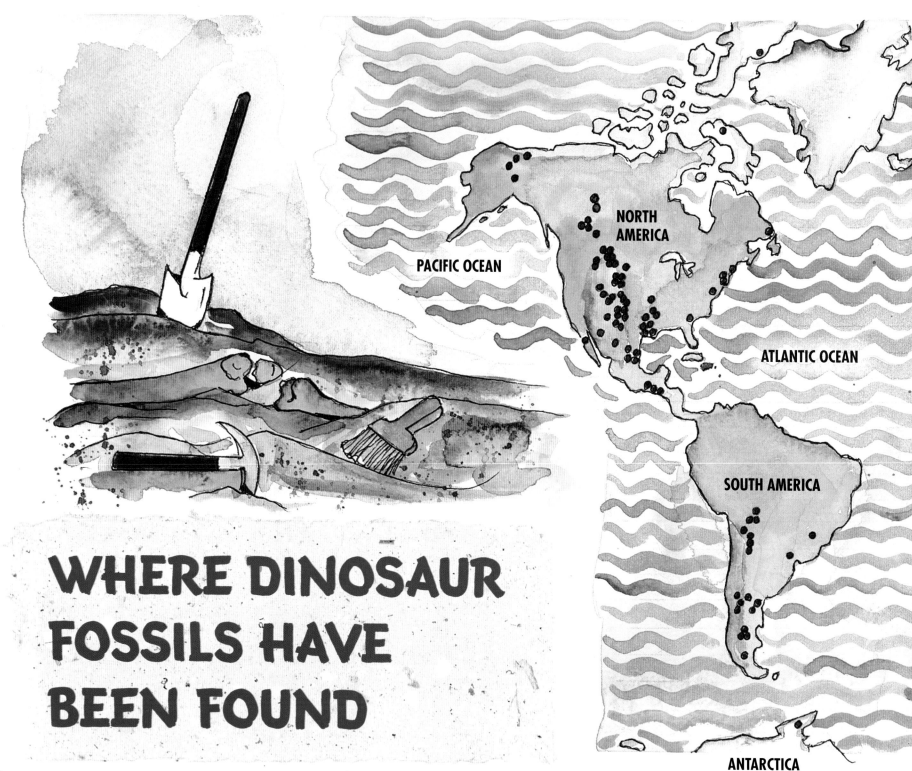

WHERE DINOSAUR FOSSILS HAVE BEEN FOUND

PACIFIC OCEAN

NORTH AMERICA

ATLANTIC OCEAN

SOUTH AMERICA

ANTARCTICA